Fall And Response

Mary E. Weems.

AFRICA WORLD PRESS
Trenton | London | Cape Town | Nairobi | Addis Ababa | Asmara | Ibadan | New Delhi

"Fall and Response" is dedicated to my late daughter Michelle Elise Weems, my husband James E. Amie, Jr. and my late poet-sister-friend Margie Shaheed (*miss you sis*)

The lines from "Black Madonna," "She is the mother of this world, the light into the next one ... to remember to keep my Blackness holy," about a Black grandmother survivor of Hurricane Katrina are haunting. "Marriage Tankas" is a probing lyrical journey through the love, joys, pains and revelatory moments discovered in remarriage when the third time around is the charm. "Lonely Tear Drops" and "Our Day Will Come" speak to the music that echoes the remembered unspoken moments in our lives. My sister-poet-friend Mary E. Weems has done it again. Fall and Response is truly a much-needed therapeutic read.

--Mwatabu S. Okantah, Poet and Chair
Department of Africana Studies
Kent State University

AFRICA WORLD PRESS
541 West Ingham Avenue | Suite B
Trenton, New Jersey 08638

Copyright © 2024, Mary E. Weems.

All rights reserved. No part of this publication may be reproduced, stored in a retrieval system or transmitted in any form or by any means electronic, mechanical, photocopying, recording or otherwise without the prior written permission of the publisher.

Book design: LiteBook Prepress Services
Cover Design: Ashraful Haque
Cover Art: Original Quilt by Mary E. Weems
Cover Art photographed by Michael Oatman
Photographs for the 7 poems in the Interior by Damien McClendon

Cataloging-in-Publication Data may be obtained from the Library of Congress.
ISBNs: 978-1-56902-861-2 (HB)
        978-1-56902-862-9 (PB)

CONTENTS

Black Madonna   1

SECTION I

Marriage Tankas	5
Night Before	6
Wedding Day	7
Wedding Night	8
Morning	9
Footnote	10
Anger	11
Rescue	13
Breast Lump	14
Recitation	15
Heart Surgery	16
Pickup Lines	17
October	18
Lonely Teardrops	20
Our Day Will Come	21
Writing Lesson	23
The Master Plan	24
Grandpa (1916-1978)	26
Washing Dishes by Hand	27
How Old Are You?	28
Breast Milk	29
Because I Could Not	30
Lament of the Urn	31
Pisces	32
Rain	33
Ice Sculpture	34
George Floyd's Mama	36

Fall And Response

Shopping While Black	38
Tracks	39
Blue Heron Sonnet	41
Dress Rehearsal	42
The Thrill is Gone	43
Target Practice	45
Survival Story	46
Head Trip	48
"Stay With Me"	50
Dis-Order	51
Suicide	52
Shit From Shinola	53
Monkey Business	54
I had a Dream	55

SECTION II

Love	58
Heart Bop	59
What I Really Want to Say About Love	61
How to Catch Cancer as a Couple	62
First Lesson	63
What's in a Name?	64
Make Room for Daddy	65
Rental Property	66
Mirror/Mirror	67
Two Black Girls at the Bus Stop	68
"My Name Is Danisha"	69
Mouth	70
Re-Raped	71
Operation Solo Haiku	72
If You Hear Something	73
Woman's Tears Trump Justice	74

Contents

Obama Out!	75
"Look at My African American Over There"	77
Abort	78
Transgender Note	79
Passing	80
Untied States	81
Segregation	82
Nurse Resurrection	83
The Last Sound	84
Fall and Response	85
Flight Lesson	86
Hope	87
The Seventh Day	89
Epilogue:	90
What the Slave Mother Said	90
Acknowledgements	92

Contents

We Fall down but we get up
From: "We Fall Down but we Get Up," Lyrics
by Donnie McClurkin

For women…poetry is not a luxury…It forms the quality of the light within which we predicate our hopes and dreams toward survival and change…The farthest horizons of our hopes and fears are cobbled by our poems, carved from the rock experiences of our daily lives.

From: Sister Outsider: Essays and Speeches by Audre Lorde (1984)
The Crossing Press, Freedom, California
The Crossing Press Feminist Series

BLACK MADONNA

> *Hurricane Katrina Relief Website
> September 7, 2005

I see through her Black eyes
an evolution of mistakes
disguised as prepare, purpose
don't piss on me and say it's raining.
This is not news, yet in the media names,
faces, scatter like buck shot on the screen, every
shade of black doing all the looting, holding all the *help us,
help me* signs on rooftops floating like waste
in the sewer--

Look up in the sky! it's nary a bird.
Pain stares ahead for help riding by
in military camouflage, in air conditioned
units—drinking bottled water, waiting
for orders
while dead babies-children-mothers-people
rot in the streets like road kill.

For days my words have been silent,
numb as a hard held hand, a child standing
in a corner for hours, hard as hate—*too late
too late, too late* repeats so long
I try to make up a song.

Fall And Response

I am this Black grandmother's eyes, an image

on a relief sight, her grandbaby
strapped to her back sleeping as if all is well
and for the infant it is. She can't see granny's dark skin
tremble to the chin, her pressed mouth, a view
no one could make up, can't see her mama's missing
in the floodwater
can't see that because their faces are Black
they've been left waiting in the back of the bus.

This elder's picture brings a thousand words
rushing, my blood mixes with hers
my anger opens like a fresh bruise
Black people used as un-wanted poster children
for tragedy, immersed yet waiting for water,
look up—wonder where the yellow went.

She is the mother of this world,
the light into the next one, wise as all women
together. She teaches me without speaking
to listen carefully for the sound of hope
humming in her granddaughter's ears,
to remember to keep

my Blackness holy.

SECTION I

MARRIAGE TANKAS

For: James, on our 10ᵗʰ anniversary

Fall And Response

NIGHT BEFORE

Sleepless. I fall through two
previous marriages. Wake up.
Cold sweat. Then calm. I remember
why I said yes to James, giggle,
try on my dress.

Section I

WEDDING DAY

The Limo is white.
We are groomed and on time.
Graceland waits like love.
We embrace the minister,
dine at the top of our world.

Fall And Response

WEDDING NIGHT

There is only one night
vibrating with single stars.
We name each one *joy*,
dance on the dark of the sky,
memorize our light two-step.

Section I

MORNING

The back of your head
rushing out of our driveway
highlights ears shaped
like the coffee cup you left
half gulped, on my moist back.

Fall And Response

FOOTNOTE

All of the drawers
and doors you opened watch.
I follow your steps.
Mumbling about messiness,
I caress each place you left.

Section I

ANGER

When the clock strikes one,
we say more than we mean. Hurt,
you leave without eyes...
Home before the clock reads two,
we say what we mean together.

Fall And Response

Section I

RESCUE

My car sits alone
in the lot like a left child.
Your truck is a steed.
I carry poems from the kids,
read them as you change the tire.

Fall And Response

BREAST LUMP

Inside I practice
living alone in Death's house.
I say *I'm not afraid,*
you sit staring still as stone.
Your sudden tears on my t-shirt.

Section I

RECITATION

Your secret desire
spills from your mouth in a dream.
Asleep you recite McKay's
"If we must die" and the audience
applauds forever.

Fall And Response

HEART SURGERY

I walk to your bed
holding my own hand. You start
ask, *Are you alright?*
I rush to answer: My lips
kiss your smile, my eyes flowers.

Section I

PICKUP LINES

My husband exits his red Ford.
Something about the way he stands, cocks his head,
lifts one black-khaki-work-pant leg at a time, makes
me want to bend on one knee, ask him to marry me.

I think of the moods of love in a single day,
the way we can be quiet, hold hands,
how he can piss me off,
make me want to kiss.

Fall And Response

OCTOBER

Fall woke me
weeping steadily
on roof's face
pooling in husband-keeps-clean gutters
watering grass seed he planted
last Sunday while I trimmed our bushes.
Our streetlamp casts sun
Whenever I move   he turns
on other side to sleep.
I listen to him breathing
as mind wanders outside
to gutter of the unkempt house
on opposite corner   caked
with weeds and dropped leaves
something that bugs husband
at least once a day.
I wade in wet dirt
stick toes in mud
leave holes
drift back   wrap my arms
around his chest
hear him muttering
in his dreams
something about water.

Section I

Fall And Response

LONELY TEARDROPS

*Jackie Wilson

A recent viewing of a years-ago commercial
about littering ends with an actor as the Indian man
his single tear
the unforgettable loneliness
on his face
reminds me of what I've learned
about tears:
Like fingerprints
they only happen once
reveal unique patterns
based on person's mood
each heart its own moon

tear ducts birth place
of blues drops, burst into,
kind that begins slow like a dance
sad ones that pool and puddle
fall in tiny oceans.

Section I

OUR DAY WILL COME

>*Lyrics by: Bob Hilliard
>Sung by: Ruby and the Romantics, 1963

Eight years old, I learned the words
to a song mama listened to over and over
as music that would take her to God.

I still remember all of the words,
that mama used to drink beer and cry
by the portable 45 record player
when she listened,
that she only played it at night after I was supposed to be in bed,
how I felt watching my mother weep about the kind of love
she didn't have, but wanted so bad:

Our day will come, and we'll have everything (whooo, oooo)
We'll share the joys, falling in love can bring
no one can tell me that I'm too young to know (young to know)
I love you so (loooove you so)
And you love me…

We never had a chance to see Ruby and her crew croon,
but close my eyes and I can still hear their voices
in our living room, the slight scratch of the needle as mama
carefully sets it back on the first groove
to play it again.

Fall And Response

Section I

WRITING LESSON

Long before I wrote my first poem
fascination with pens made me watch
carefully when mama couldn't get a pen to write.
She'd stick the tip in the metal door of the small, round
furnace in the front room then run it across the white paper
on the table until ink turned into words.

I had the bright idea to try this with a fountain pen
mama had gone out to run a quick errand
sisters and brother were playing outside.
I took the tip of the fountain pen
stuck it inside the fire door
immediately felt a burn on my finger
threw the pen forward where it hit the thin curtains
in our front room window
which burst into flames.

More scared of mama than the fire
I rushed to hide in our bedroom closet
sat there on the floor listening
as the fire department came and went
while I held my breath until mama
snatched the door open
hugged me tight without a word.

Fall And Response

THE MASTER PLAN

1.
30 years passed in drinking

and drinkers
same conversations lingering
in smoke-filled then
smokeless air
its owner
my father
posed at the end
of the bar

watching the door
watching his money
waiting for Sunday.

2.
Outside snow covers city like frosting

my father on his way to hospice
after a fall at home:

Stopped his heart
Stroked his brain
Stopped him from being able to swallow.

Section I

Winter's the season for loss
Tennyson poems.

Ice-covered streets
stretch like funeral processions

my spirit a mirror
reflecting the man who gave me his stance
business sense
smile/eyes.

3.

Daddy's body is throwing him out
his heart half-pumped
vibrates

hip fractured
like his speech.

We lean in to catch each word
try to shape sounds into sentence
watch his eyes for clues to what's on his mind
packing in the dark.

R.I.P. 2-23-18

Fall And Response

GRANDPA (1916-1978)

Lived his whole life in work clothes, long johns in winter, a hat.

Stingy brimmed, dark grey felt, 2-inch black band in the spring, fall and winter,
an almost yellow straw, narrow dark blue band in the summer.

Bald, smoked filter-less camels, drank red, Wild Irish Rose from brown paper bags he hid from granny.

Ever lose someone you loved so much
you can still hear them breathing
32 years later?

Grandpa never entered a church, lived his life like a prayer.
Gave his wife, kids and us grandkids most of his time, most of his money, most of himself.

Space he left lonely
as an unlit streetlamp.

Section I

WASHING DISHES BY HAND

Granny washes dishes in our kitchen
sleeveless, cornflower blue house dress
trimmed in plaid
always busy hands dipping deep in water
her thoughts
some secret
some about Duffy
her husband of 42 years.

30 years later, I rush to sink,
wrap my arms around her waist
hold on tight to 1988
before she died of breast cancer.
Feel my own hands alone in the suds
finishing our dishes.

Fall And Response

HOW OLD ARE YOU?

*July 13, 2022

Took me a year to cry after granny died.
Day after day grief showed up
re-entered   made me cold to the touch
difficult to be around
my concentration kind today's kids have.
I think about her everyday   not like it's a job
but a joy   every moment spent   treasured
missed   wanted back   celebrated
as if it's always her birthday July 13th
1914.

Section I

BREAST MILK

When I was growing up milk shortages
only lasted long enough for mamas
to replenish
      two   breasts
      designed   by God and his angels
      to provide the best food any baby
      can drink   my time with my daughter
unforgettable as her birth   I remember when what's natural

began to shift to what's convenient   as if life
only matters if it doesn't take up too much time
as if there's something more precious.
Even though I've long ago been out of breast milk
the idea that a government that loves to tell anyone
who'll listen that it's the greatest, bestest, richest, mos-powerfu—super
califragilistic expealidocious country in the world
has run out of formula, didn't know this was coming,

This morning, I heard a story about a desperate white woman who reached
out to a breastfeeding woman and asked if she'd share her milk
and suddenly, I'm crouching near a cabin close to the big house
on a plantation...
watch an ancestor-sister with a white baby on each knee
breast feeding.

Fall And Response

BECAUSE I COULD NOT

Daughter's suicide makes Death
arrive suddenly
in his black cap, high heeled shoes and mask
dagger in his waist
so, when he arrives, he can offer it
to me like a gift.

I imagine what it was like back
by the dark blue dumpster
alone as one dying breath
planned gun in her hand
feel the black circle
on her temple right before.

Section I

LAMENT OF THE URN

after Deborah H. Doolittle

I wish the ash I carry could come again,
reshape each flake inside its mother's house.
It's been two years, yet everyday
she lifts me up, as if her child is peering out.
When people come and sit around her table,
they never notice me behind their heads,
or that no matter what the season,
there are no flowers floating in my stead.
On bad days, in too-early mornings,
she walks barefoot to kiss my lid,
as if it is a forehead,
then stand there crying
in the leaving dark.

Fall And Response

PISCES

Since daughter's death
our home is an aquarium
all kinds of fish
toting their own water
me and husband
opening doors outside
for air.

Section I

RAIN

Because
Clouds need jobs
World needs a bath
People weep
Bad days need moisture
Weddings need bad luck
Funeral cars need a last-minute wash
Sky needs something to hold onto
And to let go of.

Fall And Response

ICE SCULPTURE

      Outside my office window is one giant black tree
every dead Black man I've ever known here   under a pale blue
white-fast-moving cloudy sky.   It's covered in all the icy tears   they
    weren't
               allowed   to shed when below with those of us
still breathing racism with the air   creating and cussing   soldiers
    struggling
                        teaching
                        and tiredz
                        of singing
                 We Shall Overcome.

Section I

Fall And Response

GEORGE FLOYD'S MAMA

Mama's an African word.
When I heard George Floyd's
shout, he took me
all the way back
to how we got here.

Back to most of our first words,
how we learned to speak,
walk, hold hands, cry.

I watched Black man, blood,
brother, on his stomach,
say please, say I can't breathe
Sir

the white knee disguised as blue
on his neck, cop's hands in his
pockets as if relaxed, as if all is well,
as if that's not a man
trapped on the ground
for eight minutes and forty-six seconds.

Section I

(Cont'd)

I realized this cop would not
have done this to a dog.
His exception so natural,
it didn't occur to him to let up
when Floyd begged for air,
his polite desperation ignored
by three cops who stood around
as if watching a movie,
without the popcorn.

It is broad daylight.

People are witnessing and recording,
when Floyd screams
and his dead mama comes
to pick him up,
as God releases him from his body
so, she,
can take him home.

Fall And Response

SHOPPING WHILE BLACK

 *May 14, 2022, Tops Supermarket

I'm sick of everything I've ever read or heard or written
about the mass shootings of Black people by white folks
Prayers and condolences to the family ring hollow
to the children of the elder Black woman
who stopped at Tops on her way to see her husband
who has been in a nursing home with Alzheimers
for the last eight years.
I watch the son who stands at the microphone
during press conference number ad nauseum
holding back tears as he talks about his mama,
her love for their daddy, his for her, tells that she used
to go and visit their father every day, that they don't know
what to do now, haven't been able to tell him yet
that the love of his life won't be coming to hug him, hold his hand,
watch their favorite TV shows, put lotion on his ashy
feet and legs—pray with him.

Section I

TRACKS

*Inspired by Lot's Wife, Anselm Kiefer, 1989

After the car accident broke mother's back,
Take two every 4 to six hours for pain
little bottles of pills filled our medicine cabinet
the toothpaste, mouthwash, razor blades,
shaving cream, moved to make room. Soon
every school day started with pills instead
of breakfast, mine always late and cold. First
time mother didn't pick me up, I walked home
to find her asleep on the kitchen floor, frozen bag
of corn she'd taken out for dinner melted, bottle
of pills sitting on stove like a pot. Months later,
I've learned to drive when she stops at red lights,
falls asleep at the wheel, keep one couch pillow
and one of her hats in the back seat, so, I can look
like I'm old enough to drive. One morning, I
stopped behind the kitchen wall, listened to mother
beg her doctor for more tell him she was still in kind
of pain I knew was a lie, her scream when he refused,
loud enough to wake our neighbor who ran to our
unanswered door, mother withdrawing on our kitchen
floor, me helpless as our cat, asking how I could help.
After that, the names changed on the bottles, then
the bottles disappeared, as she ran out of favors,

Fall And Response

most of her friends in some kind of pain. Mother
started spending more and more time in the bathroom,
telling me to pee outside or go next door when I
couldn't wait. She'd let me drive myself to school,
give me errands to run, some time getting me home
after dark, mother with a different man each day,
the tracks in their arms worn and brown, like the ones
for trains.

Section I

BLUE HERON SONNET

    For: Gil Scott Heron

He arrived suddenly like jazz, like a
Bopped Bird song, like love—naked as verse.
Raised between the North and South, at war
with himself and every shade of white pow(d)er.
Tracked truth where it lived in disguise.
Music a Valentine, Black bullets, drums.
Government hatred a constant refrain.
His life a short road map, no rainbows.
Revolution elusive as one love,
hip hop, chance of Black life on white moon.
Sixty-two the number for solitude,
bold face aged too soon, mouth, eyes glisten.
He left yesterday on a Black sunrise.
Took twenty-eight minutes to arrive.

DRESS REHEARSAL

    For: Calvin McClinton (1950-2021)

A full-length drama
everything about him flair, stylish, funk,
his lanky medium brown body stepping into new work
wisdom always seasoned with the wonder
and surprise of a child.

Our connection short and forever.
He directed my first one-woman show about being Black
in the 90s.

Opening night unwelcome ex shows up with flowers.

In the midst of our pre-show prayer in a circle
my friend looked at my frown and said "use that tonight"
teaching me with three words
to incorporate hurt feelings into character
giving it a stroke of real like a hand.

Section I

THE THRILL IS GONE

    B.B. King, Dead at 89

To be a Blues genius
you got to be born
with whatever you gon' use in yo' hands

You can't sing somethin'
you nevah had
his chords singular, Lucille
his first love arching her back
as he played
their conversation
a lifetime.

Fall And Response

Section I

Right after our Ohio governor quietly signed Stand Your Ground
into law and Conceal Carry Weapon licenses were eliminated,
I learned about a new fad—virtual gun shooting ranges

TARGET PRACTICE

the ad showing young white kids and their parents
having a ball in a safe, colorful environment touted as cheaper
than using real bullets but just as effective.

Fall And Response

SURVIVAL STORY

*Robb Elementary School, Uvalde, Texas

(*Whisper*): I'm so scared.
All our faces pointed down
I can smell wax on the floor
I count tile squares
try not to think
    about
        my best
friend who   is dead on
        number 10
make myself breathe in and out
careful
quiet
I hear girl   doing what police
        taught us to do
and mommy and daddy told me not
to do   she cries 'Help'
and the   killer comes in our door
        shoots her
so much blood
I stain my skin
Pretend   I'm   dead.

Section I

Fall And Response

HEAD TRIP

(Terrence Crutcher, 40, Tulsa, Oklahoma)
When my vehicle broke down
I was waiting for help
expecting to be home in time
for lunch dinner love a night's sleep
my own bed
but like Don Cheadle said I fit
her description
she white, blue and shouting
HEY…………………….my hearing weak
as a distant radio wave tries to bring her
in—HEY I…………...STO……………..I'm terrified
prosthetic eye tries to see
I try to obey but can't—HEY………………the rest
is listening under water and I try to look
non-threatening, to move so I don't look
like I'm going to do some/thing—HEY
…………POLICE!………………I already know this
am confused wondering why she doesn't smile
or look helpful
understand that I haven't broken
any laws.

Section I

(Cotinued)

my mind starts blaring S-O-S
S-O-S S-O-S
for a moment I think she can hear because
for the first time she looks me in the eye
so, I try to smile
but when her eyes widen—saucers
I know I've seen that look before
I know she's afraid
that I'm in trouble
I open mouth to speak
sound won't sound
what I want to say
I raise hands high
surrender/walk
toward my car to put my hands
against it, but she shoots me anyway
bullets muffled as her voice
when I drop.

Fall And Response

"STAY WITH ME"

(Philando Castile, 37, Father of Five, Falcon Hts. Minnesota)

Watching the video
his girlfriend beside daughter behind
recording live
him bleeding
traffic stopped for a broken taillight
a story cop will tell
long after this Black man
who obeyed the rules bleeds out
his legal gun still in its safe place
in his car
the arm that announced then reached
for his wallet
murdered by cop
dotted with blood of hundreds
slaughtered Black men
cover him like a shroud
as his woman
loves him to death
declares *us* innocent to a Lord
she still believes in while
spirit-hands add his name
to list written in wind
as she whispers
Stay with me.

Section I

DIS-ORDER

>   *Brad Hettinger who even burned his house down

Once you've been drowned
in war, no amount of Home
means *at ease*
streets stretch like land mines
anyone resembling the current enemy
Attention!

Each hour, the middle of the night,
days, a series of attacks played out in heads
that learn to keep their mouths shut.

U.S. always surprised when one soldier,
tired of waiting, cleans his weapon
after an argument over dinner, returns
to his in-law's house kills wife,
mother-in-law, his two children—
himself.

Fall And Response

SUICIDE

Not-so-young politician can no longer come
unless he has a gun to his head.
First request to his wife led to divorce.
Single, he used prostitutes
willing to let him play victim
for enough money to pay their rent
Once elected
He thought............................
years he spent as a gun lobbyist
would disappear
food would taste better
sense of touch, taste, smell return
instead, he realized after months of trying
to have sex with his girlfriend
that his relationship with guns is required.

Section I

SHIT FROM SHINOLA

    For: Ralph Northam
    Governor of Virginia

How many times do you have to put black shoe polish
on your face, to know it's bad for white skin
when it's made for shoes?

In 1984, Brown vs. Board was 30 years old and you were 25
Virginia's first Black governor one year away
the photo in your medical school year book
as carefully selected as any senior's

your inability to remember as much a disguise
as your Blackface.

Next day's news you apologize,
day after it wasn't you, the story you tell of winning
a Michael Jackson dance contest,
the reporter's request prompting you to look for space
to moonwalk, saved by your wife

who rings like a bell to stop your other foot
from beginning to slide.

Fall And Response

MONKEY BUSINESS

Serena Williams is one-half of a Black tennis dynasty
sisters who dominated in spite of racists refs
un-fans   games decided against/based on putting her in place
she refused to occupy   long time sheroes
I kept waiting for them to get
multiple promotions and endorsements designed
to capitalize on greatness.

Finally, an ad. Serena   all white sheets   pillow cases
stretched out as if asleep   and close by her side
in bed   a stuffed brown monkey
only one in this series of mattress ads
of white women sleeping alone.

Section I

I HAD A DREAM

Last night I dreamed
The Second Amendment died
he was dragged from his mansion in Oz
where he long ago seceded the Wizard.
The children of America tired of waiting
for adults to act—
organized on a private twitter
used their lunch money and allowance
to locate The Second Amendment
crawling out of his bedroom
late at night
drag him by his hair
to his own dungeon
where they surrounded him
and prayed
until he finally stopped breathing.

SECTION II

Fall And Response

LOVE

I keep trying to get him to take herbal pills
he has no interest in

worry daily about places in his arteries
forced open by man-placed mesh

each winter I buy him gloves
he never wears

nights I wait till he's fast asleep
memorize his snoring patterns
kiss his head
take off his glasses
clean, then put them where I know
he'll reach for them

pray each day he'll out live me
so, I don't have to remember
what it was like to be alone
in the dark.

Section II

HEART BOP

Holding heart in hand is a good way to catch the blues,
defined different by each person who catches what they can't
get rid of. No medicine for bad luck, for heart stuck in one place
like a gearshift on a truck going downhill. Once caught, blues
gets in everything like salt. Leaves small wounds in blues notes
everywhere but where you're looking at the moment.

I'll hold out my hand and my heart will be in it

Worst way to try and get rid of the blues
is to fall in love. Right at the moment you think
you've found man who has the answer
you find out he don't know shit either and what two of you
don't know put together can kill. Whoever said
what don't kill you makes you stronger lied. Don't do
no good to repeat clichés when man you love just put
your heart back in hand and left.

I'll hold out my hand and my heart will be in it

Fall And Response

After a while blood begins to dry on palm,
you miss the beat, take a chance, put heart
back where it belongs, make up a new blues
song that rhymes, contact every man you ever
thought you loved, sweet talk to get one's attention,
tell him a story about you with a happy ending.

I'll hold out my hand and my heart will be in it

Notes:
1. A 'bop' is an African American blues form created by Afaa M. Weaver
2. The refrain is from "For All We Know" by Donny Hathaway. Atlantic Recording Company, 1990.

Section II

WHAT I REALLY WANT TO SAY ABOUT LOVE

I used to know more about sorrow than love
my face in the mirror unrecognizable
mornings after, blood on the walls,
torn sheets, followed by heartfelt apologies
from teared up eyes, bouquets of flowers,
make up sex on demand.

When love finally came, I kept calling it something else,
pushing it out of my heart like a disease
drinking to drown it
circling around it like a wolf on the hunt
until a Gemini took me out
one date leading to the next,
twenty years and counting.

Fall And Response

HOW TO CATCH CANCER AS A COUPLE

She was conservative Baptist
didn't believe you needed to shout for Jesus
Black as she was.

Her husband an atheist who came home
from 'Nam with PTSD in suitcase
he never opened.

War memories released in cigarette after
cigarette, straight liquor and punishment
for his wife and daughters
who used to pray in secret he'd stay out
long enough

for something that never happened.

Section II

FIRST LESSON

The older I get the more single memories
fade like bright colors left in the sun too long
but I still remember mama's hands framing each foot
as she held my shoe steady
while I tied it alone for the first time.

Fall And Response

WHAT'S IN A NAME?

Long before I ever heard of Shakespeare or got my first rose,
I was given a name that's followed me all of my life,
first uttered by my late uncle Butch, who took one look at me
lying in mama's arms and thought I looked like a brown, sugar 'Cookie.'

Couple this with "Route 66," a popular TV show
featuring a white boy named "Cookie," (pronounced Coo-kie)
who loved to take time each episode, to carefully comb
his Brill creamed hair.

Next, my cousin Dickie who we always called 'uncle,'
saw me at one of our 4th of July Family Reunions
and either made up or repeated something he'd heard somewhere
singing: *Cookie, Cookie, lend me your comb* then sang my response
Sorry baby I left it at home.

After that the name and this stupid song followed me
like an old childhood photo,
you don't want anybody to see.

Most of my family still call me Cookie, decades after I grew up,
the show went off the air, years after my 'uncle' died,
dividing my life into two camps—
family who still think I should be served with ice cream
and everybody else who calls me *Mary*.

Section II

MAKE ROOM FOR DADDY

I am the only child of my mother and father
landing in her flat belly, a surprise at sixteen,
unprotected sex apparently had with confidence
that nothing would happen.

My dad's side practical, their plans for his life immediately after high
    school
in two years, already written in the family bible, place his mama marked
every important event.

They offered to pay for an abortion illegal,
expensive and more dangerous than childbirth,
but at sixteen, mama knew she wanted me and her parents
wrapped their love around her/us
and fell out with daddy's side forever.

People like to talk about how time flies, but that's a lie.
It's only when you're looking back with a forgetful eye,
not remembering the long days of life, working jobs you hate,
all the time spent waiting like I used to wait for daddy.
In memory, I'm always 5 years-old, dressed in pale lavender ruffles,
Black patent leather Buster Browns with grosgrain bows,
my petticoat snagging on the wooden step in front of our one-floor
apartment on Quincy. Watching the sun move my shadow
as I held my need to go to the bathroom
long as I could.

Fall And Response

RENTAL PROPERTY

I've rented all my life.   *Mama, we got to move again?* Slap...
Hold hand.   Me and my brother
his t-shirt on backwards.   Another white man
landlord.   Always answers phone when rent is due.
One-night bed bugs   bite everything.
Mama cries   asks for exterminator.
We stay up   Wait weeks   Then cat hops
With bugs.   We move out.   Mama owes
Rent.   Ex-landlord calls every day now...We
Grow up.   Mama dies behind.   Billy buys
house with wife.   I move twenty-five times
in twenty-five years.   Keep rent receipts in box
that gets big.   At night I   sit on somebody's else's
porch.   Watch the moon   like mama's coming back.

Section II

MIRROR/MIRROR

Even though circumstance
and decades of millions of cuts have separated me and mama
I'm never without her.
Every time I open my mouth
I hear her voice
When I write/inherited talent
puts her hand over mine
a perfect fit
When I walk barefoot
I see her feet
and any time I look in a mirror
it's her reflection
looking back at me
just under my skin.

Fall And Response

TWO BLACK GIRLS AT THE BUS STOP

School's let out
high school students
like bees around bus stops
on sidewalks, sharing space
with adults puzzled by this energy shot
that bounces like handballs into air.

I'm road bound. Car moves toward yet another
full day rendezvous, middle 50s marks my face
in laugh lines that stay. I catch a glimpse of me
a teen in contemporary clothes, shoes, purse,
eyes so identical for a moment I'm lost
in hand mirror.

I almost look away till they catch me, catch me—
two girls, casual as their clothes say goodbye,
lean forward natural as two people shaking hands
and kiss, kiss on the lips.

Section II

"MY NAME IS DANISHA"

> From: *Pushout*: The Criminalization of Black Girls in Schools
> By: Monica Morris

She's matter-of-fact
self-description delivered
like list of groceries
made every week
eyes too wide open
to be eleven
her stance imitates
what she thinks a grown woman is

She's only eleven but
already thinks she knows
how to ho

She's only eleven
Cherry sold for one day's
rent money
knows how to make it pop
for the first time
again

Too young for a period
she keeps a secret journal
of days/time/actions required
and how much she earns
in back seat of an abandoned car
on first street behind the schoolyard
while her books watch
from front seat
learning a lesson.

Fall And Response

MOUTH

I live on the men's room mirror
in this coffee shop.

Big, red and partially open,
I'm a mystery which keeps them
coming inside for a look,
as they find themselves imagining
the rest of me long after their hands
are dry.

Section II

RE-RAPED

Military Air Force Officer
testifies in court
both eyes drowning
she refuses to let a tear drop

she tells of violation she's been carrying
for decades
her voice measured
she speaks of shame
of feeling powerless
of being treated like a target by her commanding
officer—

First-woman fighter pilot serving in a world made for men
her battle worse than combat
where she at least had weapons
to defend herself.

Fall And Response

OPERATION SOLO HAIKU

Brain Surgery. Patient
Man plays guitar and sings
with an open mind.

Section II

IF YOU HEAR SOMETHING

I was standing in line behind a middle-aged white couple
waiting for our Chinese host to lead us to separate but equal tables
for lunch.
It was the height of the rush for lunch on a Friday, I was off and relaxed
looking forward to their hot soup and a meal
I could enjoy with a book.
I'd been socially-woke to other cultures for years by then,
well aware of what applied racism can do to people
who'd already contributed to the solid wealth foundation
of a slowly less white America, but
when the white man in front of me lost his patience, snapped his finger,
spoke in the broken English he imagines all Chinese Americans speak
to call her a *chink* to her face and demand a seat—
as she led them to their table without a word
I said nothing.

Fall And Response

WOMAN'S TEARS TRUMP JUSTICE

    News Headline, Daunte Wright's
    Killer

I overstand. After all. Officer Potter was crying. Judge Chu was crying.
Officer Potter was crying; Judge was crying explaining
through tears how it was all a terrible mistake (like slavery?)
her certainty it was an error, that Potter didn't mean to do any harm,
sentencing guidelines too high for someone so innocent
whose only crime was stopping a young Black man for driving.
Terrified, she pulled gun she thought was her taser
as unbelievable to anyone who's ever held them both
as this performance is by judge whose role is to be impartial
focus on the facts, the verdict, the sentencing guidelines
instead of witnessing a white woman's tears
adding her own to come up with a total
of two years behind bars.

Section II

OBAMA OUT!

When Obama dropped that mic
with his left-handed
2-finger kiss to lips
I ran back eight years:
Late night election
screen a constant counting
until only thing I want to hear
is announced and I scream
and cry, call my grandmother out of Heaven
my husband out of his nap
even the couch jumps for joy
everybody I know on the phone
stars throw streamers from sky
all streetlamps doo wop
I try but can't sleep
till morning after
when I buy a paper
hold election in both hands.

Hours later I'm on my knees praying
for President Obama
his family
the *Untied* States of America
and what I know is coming
sure as I'm a Black person.

Fall And Response

(Cont'd)

Obama is cool
Resistance immediate
served with watermelon
basketball fried chicken monkey and devil
remarks.

Obama is cool,
talks of cooperation, compromise
working together.

If he could walk on water
some will claim
an optical illusion
even if God bears witness.

Section II

"LOOK AT MY AFRICAN AMERICAN OVER THERE"

    Donald Trump

Trump addresses a stranger
someone he identifies by continent and country
as he thinks *Black* like a child with a box of crayons
who's never used the color
who doesn't know what Black is
what white supremacy is.

It's September 3, 2016, 66 days before the election.
Trump visits a little-known Black church in Detroit
the people protesting outside shouting *Dump Trump*
the bishop who posed pre-interview
questions defending his church as a place of love
that welcomes everyone.

Trump stands in the pews
a smile that's a frown
looking around
ready to hit the ground.

At the podium
his head barely raises
as he reads
hesitating over words
he didn't bother to practice.

Fall And Response

ABORT

    *(2) The premature termination of a mission

Opinion so important somebody leaked it.
Even Supreme Court Justice Alito
without enough power to keep his words behind
heavy, dark, closed doors until he was ready
for something millions of men and women
will never accept
and the rich never have to worry about
their freedom to bear or not to bear
dictated by dollars and doctors who protest abortions
while providing them in serene sterilized private spaces
described as vacations spots to friends
and acquaintances when the woman returns.
Our mission should we accept it
to continue to fight for the freedom
of our bodies, books, speech, religion, ability, comedy, art—
to terminate the global attack
on what it means to be alive.

Section II

TRANSGENDER NOTE

I remember my transgender
colleague his revelation
at 65 a blessed answer
to lifelong alienation
breasts on a torso that was/is
a chest, long looks in mirrors,
bathtubs, beds, wondering
whose strange skin that is and why
it makes him cry?

I look deep in cisgender mirror
Imagine seeing stranger,
to look in closet full
of mismatched clothes, underwear
drawer of no, shoes wrong style,
hair for another head.

I re-hear my friend
decades of confusion over
way he described finally not-having
breasts

feel my own
completely at home
wonder how I'd feel
if they didn't.

Fall And Response

PASSING

All their life the man or woman hid the Black
waiting to escape the first time too much time is spent in sun
or an unwanted pregnancy lives long enough to reveal the truth

Or

To say someone you love, or even know has passed
sounds like they got up, got into their car
jumped on the freeway and started speeding past
every car on the road until after years and years and years
of riding, they drop dead behind the wheel.

Section II

UNTIED STATES

I read this as a typo years ago in a student's paper
in a college class on diversity aka multiculturalism
at the time it reminded me of all of the creative writing
advice I've given myself and others about way typing wrong
word can be the better one
but this morning after waking up to another full early morning
of news reports on noose found at United,
place where steel and iron are made, the three Black men
interviewed noting that it just appeared, that it was a threat,
that it was a crime their supervisor simply took down and threw
in the trash
telling them loud and clear without a word
what he thought about them.

Fall And Response

SEGREGATION

White addicts dying of Opioid overdoses
changed the War on Drugs to the Crusade to Save Every Life Possible
with increased pressure on doctors not to prescribe
Narcan available on EMT trucks
and over the counter   Counseling
clean needles and places to shoot provided
instead of ridiculously long prison sentences that end with losing
the right to vote.
All of the focus on white heroin addicts
as if the Black ones in spite of their color
are invisible.

Section II

NURSE RESURRECTION

>For: Carlos Resurrection, RN
>COVID 19 Caregiver, 12-22-2020

He is brown like Jesus was.
His raiment's topped by shield and mask
cross invisible on a chest moving from one sick brother
and sister to the next.

He carries their eyes
the silence sounded breath
hard labor.

His patients lie in beds that for some
will become coffins.

He is the last face they will ever see
and all he wants for them
is another chance.

Fall And Response

THE LAST SOUND

At first young Chinese woman
lover of violin
is willing to wait
to let brain tumors
take her

Playing and hearing her final recital
more important
music more important
than death. Then

Her woman-doctor
a former professional violinist
plays a concerto with her
in hospital room.

Later tumors removed
hearing lost
she writes on pad
I will remember

Section II

FALL AND RESPONSE

This morning's fog makes me wonder
if God's finally concerned enough to land
like a grey cloud-spirit
enter everyone at the same time.

Kind of soul search
body never forgets.

He leaves a permanent message
along with a little blood
to remind us what it means
to be human.

Fall And Response

FLIGHT LESSON

Turning my head backwards like a Sankofa Bird
teaches me to see my past present and future
as the same road
and all the streets I crawled, ran, or walked
until I arrived
nothing more than no left turn detours
guiding me back
to God
to claim my wings.

Section II

HOPE

This morning my office window
looks out on Spring as if last night
all the houses in the neighborhood
decided to work overtime on the trees
and bushes and flowers
singing original songs to make them turn
green and all the colors of the season
in time for rain that fell
in tiny droplets just after sunrise.
Tupac's advice to keep the head up
as in looking up   as in reaching up
as in never giving up   understanding
that what this world needs—

Fall And Response

Section II

THE SEVENTH DAY

Christians believe God created the world
In six days or one-hundred and forty-four hours.

If this is true
on the seventh day, God woke up at 3 o'clock
in the morning, raised Hell
kicked him downstairs
Hired the top DJ in the Cloud Club that month
to spit raps so right
all God could do was shake his behind
drink non-alcoholic champagne
make up beats with the young
Eat soul food like tomorrow
will never come
and tell his favorite Angel
to back that thang up
one more time.

Fall And Response

EPILOGUE

On Sunday, September 24th 2023, I visited the "Lynching Memorial," an unforgettable sacred space in Montogomery, Alabama conceived and founded by African American attorney, Brian Stevenson. At the entrance was an almost life-sized series of black-metal sculptures of slaves chained together, posed on a large black-metal circular floor. It struck my spirit and I sat on the ground on my jean jacket to stay in the vibe. I was touched by the face and stance of the proud Black slave standing at the front of the circle and had the feeling the slave mother holding her infant in her arms, both mouths wide open, had something to tell me. This piece finally came on the 26th:

WHAT THE SLAVE MOTHER SAID

(Scream as if you've just lost everybody you love)

When my breasts dried up
and I couldn't feed my baby
    when white man came down to let us up
    I held her up in the air for help
Instead, he took a knife from his waist
and cut……………………………
her arm
the blood leaking
on my scream
my husband rushing

Section II

toward him   stopped by five more
who fought him to the ground
shackled our necks
chained us together

not close enough to touch.
I wrapped her arm with a piece of the rag
that covers my ass
held her close
as her body turned
cold   hugged husband
with my eyes
our grief whispers
our sorrow passed from one sister
and brother to the next
all of us crying………………………………
as they forced us back down
to the bottom of the ship
and left us weeping
in the dark.

ACKNOWLEDGEMENTS

"Black Madonna" was originally published in Cultural Studies: Critical Methodologies, 8:2 (May, 2008) DOI: 10.1177/1532708607305122

"Marriage Tankas" was originally published (under a different title and form) in the anthology Awake at the End, John Panza, (ed.) (Bottom Dog Press, 2008)

"Blue Heron Sonnet" was originally published in the Handbook of Autoethnography, Jones, S.H., Adams, T.E., Ellis, C. (eds.). (Left Coast Press, 2013)

"Head Trip," was originally published in A Race Anthology: Dispatches and Artifacts from a Segregated City. Dan Moulthrop and R.A. Washington (eds.) (Guide to Kulchur Press, 2016)

"Love," was originally published in the African American Review, 2020.